HOW TO INFLUENCE ANYONE QUICKLY

Develop Instant Influence, Improve Your Charisma and Discover the Secrets of Dark Psychology and Manipulation. Learn How to Use Body Language, Eyes and Tone of Voice

I0135685

Contents

Chapter 1: Develop Mental Toughness

Developing Mental Toughness

Mental toughness is considered a skill. If you are an athlete or know someone, ask them what mental toughness means to them. Because of mental toughness, they can maintain focus on what is important and accept all the challenges that may come ahead. This, as a result, provides them with the confidence to push their boundaries, go that extra mile, and get the job done. This also opens a doorway to self-discipline, better decision-making abilities, and heightened memory.

It is mental toughness that helps a lot of successful people to set and achieve goals. These people use mental toughness to be kind and compassionate with others and lead them as a unit and a team to the ultimate goal. However, despite their success and leadership skills, they are still susceptible to manipulation. Of course, the kind of manipulation they face is far greater than the one we are used to seeing; however, the objective remains the same. What leads them to their success is their ability to use all of the above and mental toughness to identify threats, analyze both probabilities and possibilities, and come to a logical conclusion on their own. They do this every single day.

For anyone who believes they are constantly being manipulated by those around them or fears that they are vulnerable, mental toughness can fill that void. With that said, developing mental toughness is a process that takes time and dedication. If you lack commitment, it may not reap the kind of benefits you are looking for.

Mental toughness isn't just limited to entrepreneurs and athletes. You can exercise this ability in every aspect of life, whether professional or personal. To get started, there are a few core concepts you must familiarize yourself with. Bring these into practice and use these every day from here on out.

Physical Toughness

One of the biggest components you need to start working on is your physical health. The healthier and stronger your physical form is, the easier it will be for mental toughness to find its place within your mind. The reason for that is fairly logical; you put your body through an intense workout, hence increasing its endurance power. The higher your endurance, the higher your willpower, and mental toughness will become. You will be able to take on more pain and challenges and still manage to push through. Besides, it will naturally add a boost of confidence in your personality, knowing that you look good and are healthy.

Push the Boundaries

I am not suggesting that you do this every day, but I hope you will do this regularly. Push the known boundaries further by doing more than you might do on any given day. Whether it is to drink an extra glass of water, do an additional set of 10 reps at the gym, or even complete an additional task for the day that you could have postponed till tomorrow, all of that counts. Once you are in momentum, you will start experiencing significant improvements in all aspects of life.

Positivity Is Your Friend

Many situations in life may seem completely deprived of any positivity. However, let yourself know beforehand that you expect challenges and failure to come. Once you have such a mindset, you stop worrying too much and start focusing on the long-term goal instead. When you can do that, you diminish the chances for manipulators to step in and try to deviate you from your goal.
Take on every challenge, hardship, and obstacle with positivity. Instead of focusing on the downside, start by looking for the positives coming out of the situation. If you cannot find them, it is okay to change your perspective or have someone else involved to give you a fresh new angle that you may have missed on. Analyze the problem or failure from all angles, not to answer what you could've done, but to seek out what you can do that will help you avoid such situations in the future.

Chapter 2: Learn From the Best

Whatever your field of work may be, there are always those who have made it big. Instead of relying on a new so-called friend for advice and suggestions, study those who have made it to the top. See what they do in life and how you can adopt some of their tactics to fetch astonishing results within yourself and your organization. People usually fail to do this. Instead of seeking out a mentor, they prefer talking to manipulators, disguised as people you can "always rely on" because they offer advice for free.
It is okay to invest some amount in your personal development because the return you get is far more valuable than any amount of money can buy. Not only do you become a more learned person, but you get to learn from the best, leaving no room at all for those exercising dark psychology to step in and distract you.

Be Grateful

There are far too many things in life that we are blessed with. However, the funny thing is that we fail to realize most of these. Let's begin with the most obvious ones. We can talk, walk, read, understand, touch, smell, taste, and hear. We can live under a roof in the cold harsh winters or scorching summers. We can pay for our food, fuel, rent, and the clothes we wear. We have friends, and we have enemies. Some are far less fortunate and have none of those.
Start your day by telling yourself that you are grateful, and end the day by writing down 10 things you are grateful for. Continue doing this for the next 30 days, and I assure you, you'll be in for a surprise at just how much you have to be grateful for. This does two things for you.

- It fills you with a sense of gratefulness for all that you have, and helps you to fight off the feeling of "not having enough."
- It helps you feel that you have an abundance of things, a mindset that can help you achieve a lot more in life.

Those who constantly worry that they do not have enough, let me be the first one to say that you will always be stuck with that mindset. Despite having everything, you will still feel like you do not have enough. Instead of trapping yourself in that rat race that leads nowhere, come from a place of abundance by creating a gratitude journal where you can record what you are grateful for. The psychological benefits are astonishing, to say the least.

Take Responsibility

Do not run away from taking responsibility. If you do so, you are creating room for those who are trying to manipulate you or others in the process. Such people will fully exploit this gap and toss the blame around, often having someone cornered who may have nothing to do with the task.

Promote a culture of taking full responsibility for your actions. Whether the outcome is favorable or not, do not back away. Once you start doing that, everyone will know you take responsibility for your actions and yours alone.

Chapter 3: How to Spot a Lie

No matter how much a person may want to conceal the fact that they are telling a lie, there are tell-tale signs to look for that even the best liars have a hard time concealing, as they often happen without the person's control. The body naturally acts in a different and specific way when we are saying something that we do not truly believe. We have virtually no control over these subconscious actions. There are many ways to determine when someone is telling you a lie.

Why Is This Important?

You will become better at recognizing people who have lied to you in the past and can look for signs of compulsive liars in your life. As you become an expert, people will know that they cannot get their lies past you and they will avoid trying to convince you of untrue things. On the other hand, you may want to keep these skills to yourself and keep the knowledge that someone is lying to you to yourself, in order to analyze them further and further as they weave their tales.

In addition to this, we now live in a time where we are bombarded with different forms of media every hour of the day, it has become important to be able to sort through it in order to pick out the important pieces of information. Being able to discern when you are being told the truth and when you are being presented falsehood is necessary. The media will tend to emphasize the things that they would like society to focus on, and it is an important skill to be able to determine how much of it will affect your life. In analyzing the media as well as in your interactions, picking out falsehoods can save you from wasting much of your already limited time. If we are unable to detect a lie, we may spend years with a person we barely know, we may spend dollars on beauty techniques that have over-promised, we may invest time in friends who do not have our best interests at heart. These skills and techniques can be taken with you into every minute of your life from here forward.

What to Look Out For

We are going to look at the specific areas of the body that you should look to in order to find out if you are being told a lie. We will begin with the eyes, as they are very telling in this type of scenario.

1. **The Eyes**

The first body part we will look at is the eyes. The eyes can be very telling when trying to decipher the truth from a lie. People tend to shift their gaze and avoid eye contact when they are telling a lie. This is because the eyes are a very telling part of the body and this is a well-known fact. People will avoid eye contact because they fear that if they allow you to look into their eyes, they will be given away instantly. Some others will make too much eye contact, looking you in the eyes so intently as if to study your reaction and determine if you are believing them or not. Watch for unusual amounts of eye contact, especially compared to their normal. If they are usually a person that is uncomfortable with eye contact, but they are looking you straight in the eyes, or vice versa, chances are they are trying to hide something from you. The person may also shift their eyes in all different directions, searching for ways to seem more convincing. Another thing that people may do with their eyes is to close them when telling a lie. This has two benefits for them; it shields their eyes from you, and it shields them from your reaction.

2. Body Language

This person may be fidgeting with their hands or their body in general because they are feeling uncomfortable. Not seeming relaxed in their body language is a telltale sign. It is very hard to feel relaxed when trying to get away with a lie and this shows in many different ways. The person may be moving their feet quite a bit, fidgeting with an inanimate object or their hair, and will probably be unable to sit still or even prefer to stand. They may begin pacing or picking things up to occupy their nervous hands.
The person lying will demonstrate unconfident body language. This involves closing in on oneself by crossing their arms over their chest and lowering their head and their shoulders and hunching forward. This is a posture that indicates someone is trying to make the small and unnoticeable. This posture could be a subconscious action simply because they feel like they would like to disappear or leave the situation. They may seem as if they would rather be anywhere else in the world than in front of you having the current conversation. This can show in the direction of their feet or by their subtle movements towards an exit.

The person may be trying to cover up any signs of lying showing in their body language by trying to act extremely relaxed and calm. If the persons seem to be calm to the point where the level of relaxation is inappropriate for the situation, this could be a sign of a lie. For example, when someone commits a crime and is being questioned for it as a suspect. Naturally, they are afraid of being caught and they know that this may show. To avoid being exposed by their fear they will feign calmness to the point where they are the calmest person in the room, slouching in their chair and playing games on their smartphone. This gives them away as anybody would be at least a little bit scared in this situation. They may also act quite jumpy and on-edge. While these two ways of acting seem opposite each other, the type of action they choose will vary depending on the gravity of the lie they are telling. They may be shifting their head from side to side almost glancing to see if anybody is around to catch them, or frantically scanning the people they are speaking to see if they are believing what is being said.

3. Biological Changes

People's breathing may change when they are lying. Breathing is a process that goes on mostly without our conscious intervention. When we are nervous, our breathing changes on its own as a response to the brain thinking that there is some type of threat present. This can be a sign to look for when detecting a liar. If they are lying to you and they are feeling nervous about it they will not be able to control how their body changes their breathing. Look for changes in breathing as a quick and mostly fool-proof sign.

These changes include automatic sweating, dilated pupils, tearing up or crying when sad, and shaking when afraid. If a person is lying and is trying to emulate any of these emotions, we can look for signs of automatic bodily responses that accompany the emotion. If a person is lying by saying that they are feeling distraught about something, we can examine their eyes to see if they are tearing up at all. Some people can create tears on command, but their eyes and face will look very different from that of someone who is uncontrollably crying because of their strong feelings of sadness. When analyzing a person to detect a lie, be aware not to mistake the signs of fear for truthful feelings. We must be careful to determine whether their shaking hands and dilated pupils are being caused by their fear about the event that has occurred, or if it is because of their fear of being caught for it. Their fear could also be caused by the fear of lying. This can become complicated so we must use these bodily signs of fear in conjunction with other signs of a lie in order to decode the person's non-verbal communication accurately.

4. The Hands

The other is the hands. People tend to subconsciously bring their hands up around their face when lying because they are automatically trying to cover the signs of lying that will inevitably show on different areas of their face. They may be trying to cover their mouth, as it is a commonplace that shows emotion, they may cover their eyes with their hands to shield themselves from your reaction if they feel that you are not buying their lie or to hide the movements of their eyes or the fact that they will make an unusual amount of eye contact- either too much or too little.

5. The Face

This brings us to face twitches or micro-expressions as they are called. These are the small, subconscious, and virtually uncontrollable facial expressions that occur when we feel intense bursts of emotion. These will occur and show a person's true emotions that they are trying to hide. Since the face has so many small muscles, it is virtually impossible to control what goes on, especially when it comes to intense emotion. It is even more difficult to try to control our face when we are also trying to control the rest of our body and its language to cover up a lie. In some instances, people will say they feel one way when their faces will show another. An example of this is a criminal trying to cover up a lie they told to a detective investigating the case. If the criminal thinks that the detective believes their lives, their face will briefly show a happy expression. These micro-expressions can be used to solve crimes and is one of the reasons that questioning sessions like these are recorded for playback at a later time. The video can be slowed, and these quick twitches of emotional expression can be better detected. Much research can be done on these videos after people are found to be guilty so that more information can be gathered on lying and what this looks like on the body. Another way these facial expressions can be useful to us is their timing. These natural expressions normally occur and fade very quickly, especially since they are out of our control. If someone is faking an emotion, the accompanying facial expression they would consciously make will happen at a much more delayed rate than the natural expression would.

Chapter 4: Interacting With Each Personality Type

Every now and then, we try to assess and describe people according to their personality what they display in front of others. At that time, we may ask ourselves "what is a great personality?"

And we also say that their personality may be like his dad. So, in our daily routine, we might talk about human personality which creates a long-lasting impact on another person.

Furthermore, an individual's personality is inclusive of traits and patterns which clearly influence their behavior, thoughts, motivation, and emotions. Personality is that thing that drives human beings to behave as they do. However, human personality also depends upon the genetic factors which you show to the outside world.

What makes someone who they are? Each individual has their idea of what type of personality they figure. That's why psychologists have categorized human personality into various types.

Other than the professional atmosphere, there are environmental factors that can play an essential role in the development and expression of human personality. Means from childhood till adolescence how kids are brought up usually depend upon their parents and their styles. Indeed, different norms and expectations of the culture make a human personality unique and attractive.

Now, let's put some light on the major components of human personality which make a human being a perfect person:

Impacts human behavior and actions- Human personality is not just how we respond and act in certain situations. Rather, it has come up with more unique benefits according to your past experiences. This means it constrains us to act in a certain way which maybe you don't like.

Shows multiple sides- A personality is not just our behavior with others or with ourselves, but it is a combination of our thoughts, feelings, emotions, social interactions. Now, let's talk about personality traits regarding an individual which make them unique and different. These five traits act as an ingredient to make the human personality:

- **Openness:** Open people are highly adventurous and open in front of others. Indeed, they are very curious to know new things and always appreciate art, imagination, and good thinking. The main aim of open people is to add spice to their or other's life.

Apart from that, an individual who is not open has the opposite habits. They want to confine themselves to their usual behavior and habits.

- **Conscientiousness:** Conscientious people are more responsible and are well organized. These kinds of people are independent, focused to achieve their goals, and well-disciplined. Moreover, they will not backfire on any type of journey which comes in their life ever.

The people who are low in conscientiousness are more spontaneous and free-wheeling. They are very careless towards their life. This trait helps in achieving goals in school or college life and the job also.

- **Extraversion:** The people who have extraversion traits in them are very sociable, chatty, and draw energy from the crowd. They are very assertive and cheerful in social interactions.

Furthermore, the opposite of extraversion is an introvert who wants to spend time alone with less social interaction. Their nature is very shy, but they are perfectly charming at parties.

- **Agreeableness:** This trait measures a person's heart in the form of kindness. They are likely to be trusted by anyone and are very helpful and compassionate.

Opposite to that, people are cold and suspicious and do not cooperate easily.

- **Neuroticism:** These kinds of people take more tension and easily slip into anxiety and depression. One way or the other, they find things to worry about. Due to these factors, a neurotic individual is linked to bad health habits.

Types of Personalities

Have you ever considered why human beings do what they do?
Why people react to the same situation in a different way?
In your life till now, have you tried to understand anyone maybe your loved ones?
And how despite different natures you get along with people at home or work?
Every individual is unique in his own from head to toe, and despite all that, it is very surprising to recognize any person's personality. Psychologists have boxed human personality into varied categories so that it is easy to identify. Moreover, all these personality types tell us how individuals perceive the world internally and how they interact with others in different situations.
As we all are different, and this difference makes our place and life more interesting. That's why some individuals get easily successful in their life but, some take time. Have you imagined that what happens if all the persons were the same?

To understand this, let me give you an example, just imagine a house is on fire and out of many people some are rushing towards the house to evacuate it, some of them are making arrangements for the ambulance. Other than this, most of the people call the fire brigade. In this scenario, if all the individuals will do only one job, then who will do the other arrangements. This is one of the examples of varied personalities which is very crucial to handle any situation.

Every human being reacts differently in the same situations which are required to live life. We are motivated by different personalities, thoughts, actions, and reactions. That's why numerous humans choose their role models which they want to be like them.

Now the next question arises why it is essential to understand human personality?

Well from an academic point of view, it is very interesting but, if we talk about life then it is much more essential than academics. The better you understand yourself and the human beings, the more capable you become in dealing with different situations and become more successful.

Understanding human personality is a practical subject so that you maintain your life, deal with varied situations, manage the issues, and most crucially manage and understand your impact on another person's life.

So, being blind to your personality leads to these things:

- Negativity inside us remains to unlock, which becomes a hurdle in getting success.
- We only focus on our weaknesses, not on the strengths.
- You can miss the opportunity to play with your strength and improve your negative traits.

And you also need to understand the opposite person, which then leads to:

- Understanding another person, you try to interact with that according to the situation.
- While understanding the whole personality of the individual, you cannot get trapped in their first impression.

So, it would be very beneficial to understand human personality which would lead to happiness, growth, and self-development.

Chapter 5: Mass Media Manipulation

The term "Yellow Journalism" is shortened from "Yellow Kid Journalism" after the popular *Yellow Kid* comic by Richard F. Outcault at the end of the 19th century. The Yellow Kid was a bald snaggle-toothed kid in an oversized yellow nightgown who stereotyped the very poor in New York City. Sometimes making fun of the poor and sometimes making fun of the rich, the Yellow Kid became a popular and humorous political figure of the time.

Outcault was working for Joseph Pulitzer at the World when William Randolph Hearst lured him away with a large salary in order to increase his paper sales among those whose loyalties lay with the Yellow Kid. Pulitzer hired another cartoonist and created a second Yellow Kid, and the two Yellow Kids battled each other through the remainder of the century.

The line between news and entertainment has become blurry as Pulitzer and Hearst competed for the highest newspaper circulation in New York City in the 1890s. Sensationalized news stories became a norm because they drove up newspaper sales and kept Americans hungry for more exciting stories. Often, the news was altered to fit the story ideas that the editors thought would sell the most papers. Sometimes, stories were fabricated and interviews were faked. Pictures would be added to create dramatic appeal and make interesting insinuations.

While most news media today is held to higher standards of ethical reporting, that doesn't mean that it's less influential, or that a newspaper or TV station isn't concerned with circulation, viewership, and money. News media today still have the same biases and the same propensity to sensationalize what they can get away with in order to drive sales, but they must be a lot more subtle about it today.

Setting Headlines That Trigger Negative Emotions

Around the time that the Watergate scandal started to break, journalism professors, Maxwell McCombs and Donald Shaw, were coming up with a new theory of how the news media shapes our perspectives. They called it "Agenda Setting Theory." The idea is that the news media determine what news events we are exposed to and therefore what we think and talk about.

They went on to find that every news source has its own bias, even the ones that claim otherwise. NewsHour with Jim Lehrer might take a fairly moderate view on most things, but the slightly more liberal bias and framing might be enough to sway opinions on the edge more in favor of a liberal idea than a conservative one. That being the case, the news media subtly inform our opinions about different events by framing stories in a specific way. While some media sources will make a school shooting about race and ethnicity, others will make it about violent video game use or the deficits of the educational system. Depending on which newspaper you read or the program you watch, you might unconsciously find yourself assuming the subtle (or not) viewpoint of the source from which you read about the event.

The news media can make some topics more salient than others by giving them more words and featuring them more prominently than others. We take our cues about what's important in the world from what story has the most words on the front page of the paper and what the news anchors spent the most time talking about.

On the flip side, news media can make other topics less salient by saying less about them and burying them in the back pages of the paper or only mentioning them in passing on the evening news.

In addition to Agenda Setting Theory, another theory related to news and entertainment media, particularly network television, was making its way onto the scene in the 1960s. Researchers George Gerbner and Larry Gross developed the theory out of an interest in seeing what long-term effects-heavy television watching was having on people.

Interested particularly in what TV violence does to a person's perspective over time, they devised a method to figure out the amount of violence present in each primetime show and then invited light and heavy television viewers to take a series of surveys that test for the shows they watch, how much time they spend watching television, and what their worldviews are like.

Gerbner predicted that due to the quantity of violent television programming people digested every day, they would believe that the world is a meaner, scarier place than those who rarely watched TV (Griffin, 2012). Decades of research revealed that he was correct. Moreover, further analysis of his studies revealed that not only do people who watch more violent television believe that the world is worse than those who don't, but the content of the program itself influences who people believe the violence is most likely to happen to.

How Programs Get Your Reaction

Programming is paid for by advertisers, who recognize news and entertainment as vehicles to get the word about their products and services into the minds of the public. In order to win better sponsorship, networks produce programming that will most appeal to the advertisers' target audience. Higher viewership of a certain show means continued sponsorship and more money.

The Correct Use of Social Media

Social Media has indeed influenced all of us. We should use these tools to validate our resources before trusting anything presented to us. When you are presented with an unbelievable news story, check multiple sources of varying political agendas. Don't assume that once you've read one you've read them all, as you'll never be able to escape bias entirely. Even the most moderate sources overall will slant one way or another on individual stories. After all, a story with no angle is a boring story indeed.

Be vigilant about the television programming and movies that you watch. If the shows you like to watch are violent or overtly sexual in a way that portrays people inaccurately, it would be wise to limit how much you watch. Several hours of TV viewing every day will greatly affect the way you view the world and other people.

Be aware that the purpose of your favorite shows is not to entertain you but to persuade you to buy things. This warning is not made so that you derive less enjoyment from your favorite programming. Au contraire. It is made to remind you that the corporate entities paying to keep your favorite show on the air are doing so only for the opportunity to get you to buy stuff from them. Consciousness about the purpose of TV and advertising will keep you grounded and less susceptible to manipulation.

Chapter 6: NLP Secrets

What Is NLP?

NLP stands for Neuro-linguistic Programming and focuses on the language your mind speaks and how it functions. To use an example, have you ever tried to hold a conversation with someone that didn't speak the same language as you? The common picture painted is a couple going out to a fancy French restaurant. You read the menu and believe you'd ordered a soup, but instead, you're treated to a plate of liver and onions.

This scene can be used to explain what goes on within our unconscious mind. We look at the menu and believe we've put in our order for a well-paying job, a nice house, a fulfilling relationship, a happy family, and toned abs, but if that's not what ended up, then there's been some sort of miscommunication along the way. Within NLP, it's often said that your unconscious mind is the part that sets your goals, while your conscious mind is the part that accomplishes those goals. Your unconscious mind holds your deepest desires, and the truth about what you want in life, but if you don't know how to communicate this properly, then you'll always end up with the wrong menu item.

Take a common vice such as procrastination and understand your unconscious mind only acts this way because it's led to believe that's what you desire. Understanding and studying NLP is like taking that French language course, so you're able to tell the waiter, who is your unconscious mind, what you truly want out of your life. Unless you're able to communicate successfully, you won't be able to match your unconscious and conscious minds together.

NLP is a powerful tool and technique used to speak with yourself, to overcome challenges within your life. These challenges can include fears and phobias, different beliefs, and various other roadblocks created by your mind. Not only does understanding NLP make you a better communicator with yourself, but it also assists you in communicating with others. You'll be able to influence other people in your life in positive ways so that they could overcome their fears within their lives. This will also help to better their own lives.

NLP was founded by two different men by studying different therapies and focusing on modeling. They watched and observed others, breaking down the language they would use and the ability to produce a change in others. If there is a result that you would like to duplicate, you can produce the same result by breaking down the interaction. This consists of modeling different language patterns, how someone takes in information and processes it. If a successful person can accomplish amazing feats, then copying their methods should allow you to be just as successful.

We process information in multiple different ways, and a large part of NLP relies on the understanding that so that we can change it. We want to change our view on certain information, whether that be positive or negative. We also tie certain emotions and moments together that can be shifted. Numerous people have used NLP to become more motivated people in their everyday life and to be happy overall. Now that we've homed in on what NLP is, we'll give you a few tricks to make it work for you. Before we begin, let's start by saying these are only some quick tricks to help you understand and use NLP to help better your life. In order to get the full extent of NLP information, we'd need an entire book, if not multiple books, to dive that far into it. However, these methods are simple and can help you as fast as you begin to use them.

The only thing that matters within NLP is the truths you hold within yourself; another person's perception means almost nothing. Someone can tell you that your outfit looks gross, and they are operating of their definition. However, that doesn't mean that your definition must be the same; it only matters what you believe. You hold all the power within your belief, and that belief shapes your reality. Believing that your outfit makes you look like a model better serves you in your life and it'll benefit you to believe as such. This is the only bit of information that is useful to you and your life.

NLP also uses certain methods that help you break habits. Let's say that there's an action like smoking cigarettes or something you do a lot that you want to stop doing, you'd explore the Swish pattern. Despite coming up with a plan to stop smoking, and being motivated at that moment, you end up not following through. Instead, you forget the plan you've created and gone right back to lighting up another. The Swish pattern takes that idea of starting a program, like a journey to stop smoking, and gives it a new view. When you're creating a plan, you tend to think about the experience of trying to quit smoking, instead of visualizing yourself within that experience. On the opposite side, this is the root of trauma and triggers within your life, because people will snap back to that experience as if they are there. It gives you the urge to begin to panic and to act out of pure fear, instead of realizing the new situation at hand. The same thing happens when you form a plan to break a habit.

You continually break your plan and fall back into the feeling of disappointment and failure. You replace the image you continually have of failing in your goals, and you swish it with an image of yourself. Instead of seeing your failures, you see yourself as you want to be. This is powerful because most people cannot visualize the outcome and can only see the problem in front of their faces.

The swish method allows you to visualize yourself as a non-smoker and to live a happy and healthy life, on the other side of your program.

This is tremendously motivating and gives you a mental image to work towards instead of simply saying you need to quit your bad habits.

If you're only focused on not smoking so much, then you're focusing on smoking, which makes you want to smoke more. Use that mental image of yourself and keep it vague so that you can associate that image with a relatable future you. You can always swish an image of you denying a cigarette or not smoking, and it may work sometimes, but won't work all the time. Visualize yourself as a better you, overall, and you'll find the effects to be amazingly beneficial when it comes to breaking habits.

Visualizing is a powerful tool within NLP if you're feeling unmotivated, depressed, or procrastinating on something that you need to be done. Studies show that when we think of something we enjoy doing and close our eyes, we tend to view that item or action as close, vibrant, large. If you enjoy playing basketball, the visual of a basketball will be bright within your mind. In order to create motivation, you need to use this same idea, but in reverse, by bringing an image closer to you. Close your eyes and try visualizing that item or that action in your mind. Odds are, it seems far away and dimly lit, because you believe it to be out of your reach. Every person visualizes within their mind, whether they think, they do, or don't. Take the image of that action that you don't enjoy doing and visualize it in your mind. Picture the image brighter, bigger, and more within your reach and control. It may seem silly, but practicing this technique over time will change the way you view the undesired action. No longer will you become depressed at the thought or procrastinate because it feels much more within reach.

Some people rely more on auditory than on visual. However, this works almost the exact same way. When you close your eyes and think about something you hate, what kind of dialogue do you have with yourself? This dialogue can reference your inner dialogue, as well as outer. What kinds of things do you say about it? Now, imagine something you enjoy doing, and compare the two. Typically, your facial expression may even spread into a smile. For example, say you're trying to motivate yourself to clean your kitchen. Try speaking similarly to yourself when thinking of cleaning your kitchen. Change your tone, tell yourself that you enjoy it, and use empowering language. This will change any negative feeling you have to a positive one.

Another positive technique of NLP we'll cover is known as "Anchoring." Anchoring is the process of tying an emotion with an action on the concept so that you feel that emotion whenever you activate it. For instance, if you're driving in your car and see an ambulance behind you with its lights turned on. It's normal to feel a sense of dread or to feel stressed out.

If you see the lights and hear the siren again even if it's not attached to an ambulance, you'll feel the same sense of dread you had before. The image of that ambulance is anchored to that emotion. Take an example of homework and the feelings you get when looking at an unfinished page.

Those emotions have been tied to that image your entire life. This is also how advertisements take hold of your attention and incite emotion within you. Commercials with happy family gatherings may make you feel elated, and then the product flashes, allowing you to anchor that elation to the product they're trying to sell. Using this same logic to assist us can be incredibly beneficial. While you're in the midst of a happy experience, such as an event with friends, or maybe even a concert, start doing something such as snapping your fingers or clapping your hands. Choose an action that you don't do so often, it needs to be unique. When you begin to feel sad or unmotivated, begin to clap your hands or snap your fingers to incite that same emotion. Just as you can create a positive anchor, there are also such things as a negative anchor. Often, people can't get any work done within their bedrooms because of the anchor they've created. You get inside your bed when it's time to sleep, and thus, an anchor is created for sleep. Possibly, your room is where you retreat when you're feeling depressed, so you create a negative anchor for being depressed. The trick is to notice these occurrences and avoid the negative anchors while inciting positive ones.

"Reframing" is also a proven helpful technique within the realm of NLP. Imagine that every moment of your life has a picture snapped of it and put into a single frame.

You feel a certain way when you look at the picture and recall that moment in your life. Reframing speaks of taking a hold of that photo and turning it to the side to get a brand-new view of it.

Before long, you're looking at the photo like you never have before, and what really matters, you've changed how you feel about that moment, as well. For example, there's a moment in your life when you got in trouble for having bad grades in school. Possibly, you walked away from that moment feeling like you were a bad person, and that you weren't good enough to get better grades in school. Try turning the frame and giving this moment in your life some new perspective. Instead of looking at it with a negative view, think of the positives.

Chapter 7: Subliminal Manipulation

Covert emotional manipulation is used by people who want to gain power or control over you by deploying deceptive and underhanded tactics. Such people want to change the way you think and behave without realizing what they are doing. In other words, they use techniques that can alter your perceptions in such a way that you think that you are doing it out of your own free will. Covert emotional manipulation is "covert" because it works without you being consciously aware of that fact. People who are good at deploying such techniques can get you to do their bidding without your knowledge; they can hold you psychologically captive.

Covert emotional manipulation is more common than you might think. Since it's subtle, people are rarely aware that it's happening to them, and in some cases, they may never even notice. Only keen outside observers may be able to tell when this form of manipulation is going on.

You might know someone who used to be fun and friendly, then they got into a relationship with someone else, and a few years down the line, they seem to have a completely different personality. If it's an old friend, you might not even recognize the person they have become. That is how powerful covert emotional manipulation can be. It can completely overhaul someone's personality without them even realizing it. The manipulator will chip away at you little by little, and you will accept minute changes that fly under the radar until the old you are replaced by a different version of you, build to be subservient to the manipulator.

Covert emotional manipulation works like a slow-moving coup. It requires you to make small progressive concessions to the person that is trying to manipulate you. In other words, you let go of tiny aspects of your identity to accommodate the manipulative person, so it never registers in your mind that there is something bigger at play.

When the manipulative person pushes you to change in small ways, you will comply because you don't want to sweat the small stuff. However, there is a domino effect that occurs as you start conceding to the manipulative person. You will be more comfortable making subsequent concessions, and your personality will be erased and replaced in a cumulative progression.

Covert emotional manipulation occurs to some extent in all social dynamics. Look at how it plays out in romantic relationships, in friendships, and at work.

Emotional manipulation in relationships. There are many emotional manipulations in romantic relationships, and it's not always malicious. For example, women try to modify men's behavior to make them more "housebroken"; that is just normal. However, specific instances of manipulation where the person's intention is malicious, and they are motivated by a need to control or dominate over the other person.

Positive reinforcement is perhaps the most used covert manipulation technique in romantic relationships. Your partner can get you to do what they want by praising you, flattering you, giving you attention, offering your gifts, and acting affectionately.

Even the seemingly nice things in relationships can turn out to be covert manipulation tools and props. For instance, your girlfriend could use intense sex as a weapon to reinforce a certain kind of behavior in you. Similarly, men can use charm, appreciation, or gifts to reinforce certain behaviors in the women they are dating.

Some sophisticated manipulators use what psychologists call intermittent positive reinforcement to gain control over their partners. They will shower the victim with intense positive reinforcement for a certain period and then switch to just giving them regular attention and appreciation levels. After a random interval of time, they will again go back to the intense positive reinforcement. When the victim gets used to the special treatment, it's taken away, and when they get used to standard therapy, the special treatment is brought back, and it all seems arbitrary. Now, the victim will get to a place where he becomes sort of "addicted" to the special treatment, but they have no idea how to get it, so they start doing whatever the perpetrator wants in the hope that one of the things they do will bring back the intense positive reinforcement. In other words, he effectively becomes subservient to the perpetrator.

Negative reinforcement techniques are also used in relationships to manipulate others covertly. For example, partners can withhold sex to compelling the other person to modify their behavior in a specific way. People also use techniques such as silent treatment and withholding of love and affection.

Some malicious people can create a false sense of intimacy by pretending to open up to you. They could share personal stories and talk about their hopes and fears. When they do this, they create the impression that they trust you, but their intention may be to get you to feel a sense of obligation towards them.

Manipulators also use well-calculated insinuations to get you to react in a certain way at the moment to modify your behavior in the long run. People in relationships are always trying to figure out what the other person wants out of that relationship. A manipulative person can drop hints to get you to do what they want without having responsibility for your actions because they can always argue that you misinterpreted what they meant. Dropping hints isn't always malicious (for example, if your girlfriend wants you to propose, she may leave bridal magazines out on the table). However, malicious insinuations can be very hurtful, and they can chip away at your self-esteem. Your partner can suggest you are gaining weight, and you aren't making enough money or suggesting that your cooking skills aren't any good. People use insinuations to get away with "saying without saying," any number of hurtful things that could affect your self-esteem.

For example, if a friend wants you to do them a favor, instead of coming out and asking you, they go to a mutual friend and suggest that they ask you on their behalf. When a mutual friend approaches you, it becomes tough for you to turn down the request because of added social pressure. When you say no, your whole social circle now perceives you as selfish.

Passive aggression can also involve the use of silent treatment to get you to comply with a request. Imagine where one of your friends talks to everyone else but you. It's going to be incredibly awkward for you, and everyone will start prying, wondering what the problem is between the two of you, and taking sides on the matter.

Friends can also covertly manipulate you by using subtle insults. They can give you back-handed compliments that have hidden meanings. What they meant by the compliment, you will realize that it's an insult in disguise, which will bruise your self-esteem and possibly modify your behavior.

Some friends can manipulate you by going on a "power trip" and controlling your social interactions. For example, there are those friends who insist that every time you hang out, it should be in their apartment or at a social venue of their choosing. Such friends often intend to dominate your friendship, so they are keen to always have the "home ground advantage" over you. They'll try to push you out of your comfort zone just so that you can reveal your weaknesses, and you can then become more emotionally reliant on them.

Manipulative friends tend to excessively capitalize on your friendship, and to a disproportionate degree. They will ask you for lots of favors with no regard for your time or your effort. They are the friends who will leverage your friendship every time they need something but then make excuses when it's their turn to reciprocate.

Emotional manipulation at work. There are some reasons why your colleague may want to manipulate you. It could be you are on the same career path, so they want to make you look bad. It could be that they are lazy, and they want to stick you with their responsibilities. It could also be that they are a sadist, and they want to see you suffer.

One way people at work exert their dominance over others is by stressing them out and then, almost immediately, relieving the stress. Say, for example, you make a minor error on a report, and your boss calls you into their office. They make a big fuss and threatens to fire you, but then towards the end, they switch gears and reassures you that your job is secure as long as you do what they want. That kind of manipulation works on people because it makes them afraid and gives them a sense of obligation at the same time.

Some colleagues can manipulate you by doing you small favors and then reminding you of those favors every time they want something from you. For instance, if you made an error at work and a colleague covered for you, they may hold it over your head for months or even years to come, and they are going to guilt you into feeling indebted to them.

Colleagues can also manipulate you by leaving you out of the loop when passing across important information. The intention here is to get you to mess up so that they can better stand with the boss or with other colleagues. When you discover that someone is leaving you out of the loop at work and you confront them, they could feign innocence and pretend that it was a genuine mistake on their part, or they could find a way to turn it around and blame you.

People with dark personality traits tend to be hypercompetitive at work, and they won't hesitate to use underhanded means to pull one over you. Most colleagues turn out to be good friends, but you should be careful with colleagues that are overly eager to befriend you. It could be that they want to learn more about you so that they can figure out your strengths and weaknesses and find ways to use them against you. Narcissists, Machiavellians, and psychopaths are very good at scheming at work, so don't let them catch you off guard.

Chapter 8: Hypnosis Techniques

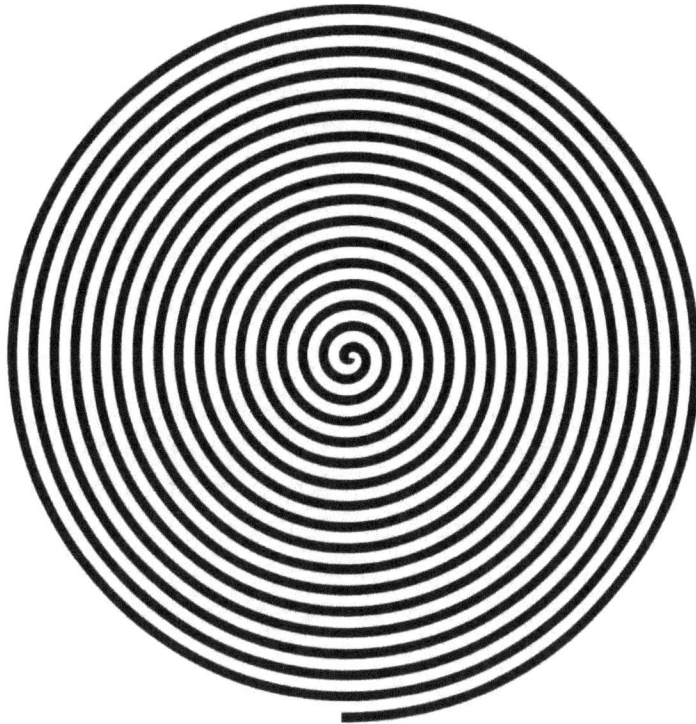

If you think of the word hypnosis what is the first question that comes to mind? The solution for many people is this: a Hollywood movie with an overly performed scene together with a hypnotherapist and his mysterious revolving watch. Around the hypnotist is a poor person who is about to be decided to send to some location in their mind they have still yet to visit in more than twenty years. The fact is, hypnosis is less effective in the modern world. Hypnosis is, in the simplest form, a type of manipulation involving reducing a person's awareness of their outer surroundings and increasing their internal attention. We react more favorably to advice while a person is under hypnosis since their rational thought is damaged. That is why the film will show a subject unquestionably responding to a hypnotist's commands.

Hypnosis has some psychology to it, so it includes knowing how the human mind functions. The human brain is built in such a manner that experiences are contained in the conscious mind that governs rational thought, and the subconscious mind. The rational mind is what advises you that it is risky and foolish to cross a busy street without looking. Whilst the subconscious brain is likely to warn you that weight loss is impossible as the images of the last time you attempted to lose weight are held in it. Hypnosis tends to work by altering and replacing the subconscious required you get about certain things with stronger and more useful thoughts.

The Misconceptions About Hypnosis and Manipulation Burst

It seems almost difficult to believe the use of hypnosis in our daily lives, but the simple fact of the situation is that it is so. You might not have had any twirling watches in your face, and during your waking hours your eyes may be constantly open, and you are most certainly hypnotized when you go about your everyday life. How could it be?

When is the last moment you read a book that really made you lose sight of what was going on around you? You were effectively hypnotized when you were in the condition of being completely immersed in your work. They assess potential are you weren't even distantly aware of people standing near you and living their lives. Really quiet, you were riding somewhere on a train, along with the main character's actions and thoughts. That is real-life hypnosis. No hypnotizers, no continues to watch your subconscious brain take a journey to an alternative universe.

Self-induced hypnosis is often normal in children who often fall into this trance many times a day at least. That's why, when they watch their special cartoon series with no reaction, you'll call your boy. They don't want to ignore you. They actually cannot understand you because they have blocked out the aware mind and the universe because they live in another realm where they are completely blocked to the subconscious. Throughout their shows, musicians and performers requiring concentrated attention to succeed brilliantly in their sport or craft quite frequently fall into hypnotic trances. Many will mention this trance as being "in the zone." What sometimes happens is that the mind of the artist is so concentrated on what they are doing, that during this period nothing else matters. Writers often get in the groove when it comes to the writing process. When this occurs, you may notice the writer being transported into the universe they've created their words with. Reluctant or unable to abandon this planet, the writer can produce thousands of words a day when, due to writer's block, they have historically been unable to venture past a few hundred lines.

Some individuals and groups have experienced suitable methods of utilizing hypnotherapy to their advantage when it comes to mind control and manipulation. Making a long speech and conducting a lengthy and almost never-ending lecture, for example, all have the purpose of bringing the listener into a trance-like area. That may be due to boredom or fatigue, or a mixture of both. If an individual is in this condition, they are more friendly and willing to sign up for anything you sell. This is something that has been mastered by many cult leaders and would understand why many cultural meetings are sometimes long and dreary. A cult meeting has rarely ended in a few mins. If you conclude a meeting in 15 minutes, the minds of the attendees will still be strong and doubting. But when you go on about for hours, they start unknowingly falling out of control and will not be as resistant to your advice as they would be in the first 15 minutes. Another tactic used to accomplish hypnosis is to present contradicting knowledge as if it were not contradictory but completely logical. What do you mean by that? There is a critical reasoning area of the brain. By helping you filter vital details, this region of the brain is just what keeps you safe and out of danger. If this area of the brain is swamped with conflicting data without adequate time being given to handle it, it closes down. When your rational reasoning has been disregarded, you are apt to follow any ideas offered to you even if they may not be agreed by a normal-minded individual in harmony with their mind's reasonable pieces.

How to Hypnotize Someone Without Them Knowing

You can use hypnosis in everyday life to obtain what you want from people without them beginning to suspect what you are up to. One positive thing about hypnotherapy as a manipulation tool is that it's subtle and leaves no evidence behind it. Except for lying where you could find yourself caught in your lies, hypnosis does not leave any traces behind. No one is going to walk up with you and start accusing you of hypnotizing them. Even in the worst-case situation, you can just be convicted of getting away from it. The first process to effectively hypnotize a person is to establish a connection with that person. You can very rarely hypnotize a random person to whom you express no connection at all. It's fairly simple to establish a link with a human. You only need to observe and react correctly to your facial expressions and theirs, and their body language as well. The entire point of creating a bond is to make sure the other individual is accessible to you and can react favorably to your overt stimulation of the mind, better known as hypnosis. Make use of some of the following suggestions to hypnotize them after being certain of the presence of any connection for both you and your subject:

Tip #1: Turn Them Away From Familiar

Humans love patterns. They are simple, straightforward, and soothing to understand. Patterns are a significant component of the comfort zone and do not require any logical thought. What patterns did you set in your life, and how do they assist you? Patterns simplify life for many. Let's consider a simple method that can be interrupted with a person's intent to hypnotize. Let's say you and your fiancé have a method of saying goodbye before work every morning, which involves a kiss on the cheek and a quick hug. You feel particularly philanthropic one morning and decide to start replacing your pattern with a tight, residual hug and a full kiss on the lips. The mind of your spouse will be thrown into chaos because that's not what mentality is used to. You'll have a short opening for a hypnotic order in the five seconds of uncertainty that will ensue in your spouse's head.

Now, you can make lasagna?

Your spouse does respond instantly, of course.

They should have sat back on every other day and remembered the labor involved in creating lasagna, and would hopefully have proposed an option. On the day you toss them off your sequence, they'll say yes without too much thinking, because you've essentially shortened their conscious mind.

Tip #2: Use the Zeigarnik-Effect

The Zeigarnik effect in psychology is the principle that consumers are more inclined to recognize unfinished tasks than the ones that have been finished. Think about all this: if you're planning to do your laundry, you're likely to have that thought persisting in your brain until you actually wash and put away all your dirty clothes. You will no matter how much experience you have any interest in memorizing everything to do with laundry soon after you have completed your laundry duties. The Zeigarnik impact was named after a Russian psychologist, who had been inspired by her professor to investigate the phenomenon. The teacher, one Kurt Lewin, made the point that the orders which were still unpaid could be remembered more precisely by a waiter.

In certain cases, Zeigarnik's influence is seen in daily life. In particular, soap operas and TV-show are eager to leave their listeners wanting more by ensuring each series ends with such a cliffhanger. When an episode runs out anticlimactically, your brain will store this as an incomplete task in your short-term memory. That's why you keep returning to your favorite soap opera because your brain knows you to complete what you begin. As far as the incompleteness lingers in your brain somehow, your mind will be attracted to it.

Try sharing an entertaining tale with breaks in between throughout which you send them hypnotic orders to hypnotize anyone using the Zeigarnik method. This may sound something like this:

You won't believe what happened when I wanted to go camping with my friends last weekend. We walked up this very desolate path when all of a surprise, we heard these odd sounds coming from the woods [could you kindly closed the door for me]. They sound like a cross between a bear and a coyote and they grew louder and louder the farther we went up the road. Of course, we're getting very worried at this point but we knew there was no going back. There were four of us, so we were able to battle everything that it was...

You may ask your dialogue companion to do fairly much whatever you like, without much resistance, throughout this storytelling. That's because their brain is centered on the story you're telling, and their nervous system is anxious to finish. They're your plastic to work with while they're in that trance-like state.

Tip #3: Stay Contentious

Ambiguity keeps a guess on your audience. If you want to stick to people's minds who you connect with even after the interaction is finished, you have to find a compromise between being unforgettable and staying vague. Ambiguity continues to keep mind-blowing. What did they mean exactly and they explained this or that? You are in the power of another person as far as their minds ask. It confuses the conscious mind with vagueness and ambiguity. There are aspects that the human mind cannot perceive and one of them is the nature of uncertainty.

Ambiguity in the world of relationships and dating can serve a vital role in persuading others to go somewhere with you and date you. Many involved personally will agree that a bit of a mystery will serve a long way to keep life interesting. What doesn't explain most is why. The possible explanation of why secret is so interesting is that as far as a person's conscious mind has not properly confirmed and understood you would always stay in their minds. By always making sure you remain vague and enigmatic regarding one or two things, you will hypnotize your friend or girlfriend into doing what you need them to do.

Chapter 9: Mind Control

Mind control is a general term that is used to define various theories that propose that a person's decisions, emotions, behavior, or thinking can be influenced. Many genres of fiction use mind control as a common plot device. The fact that it is omnipresent is perhaps unsurprising. The prospect of being able to gain full and explicit control of the mind gives rise to many startling and alluring possibilities. There are several implausible forms of fictional mind control—magical interventions, telepathy, and evil plans of authoritarian organizations. Mind control is also implemented by certain devices in more scientifically inspired plotlines where certain devices are implanted in the brain of the subject to manipulate neurophysiological processes that can cause a change of mental state.

In the real world, mind control involves various methods by which the mind can be influenced. It includes the effects that are mediated via our senses. These might include positive influences like using environmental manipulation to nudge someone to make healthy decisions or using presented evidence to update one's belief. They can also be subtler, as in the case of brainwashing or propaganda. Apart from environmental and social means, it can also be caused by direct neural stimulation. Neural stimulations can cause neural discharges through direct manipulations via brain stimulation or by subtle modulation with pharmacological agents. There has been a steady increase in the use of brain stimulation in recent decades as an aid to many who suffer from mental disorders.

What Is Mind Control?

The words "mind control" and "cult" have many misunderstandings regarding their definitions. But what do these words mean, and how can you tell the difference between being controlled into exploitation and the conveyance of a good idea?

Mind control is defined by several terms including compliance-gaining influence, behavioral change technology, sociopsychological manipulation, malignant use of group dynamics, exploitive persuasion, manipulation, and uninformed consent, thought reform, coercive persuasion, and brainwashing. Cults, on the other hand, are known by names such as ideological totalism, coercive organization, authoritarian structure, and closed system of logic. While some of these words are full of preconceived ideas, emotions, energy, and charge, others are more self-descriptive.

The study of thought reform is considered to be the study of the method of altering people's behaviors and minds through influence and persuasion. Influence is not inherently negative in and of itself. The degree to which a person is exploited and the extent of the deception used is what differentiates coercive persuasion from ethical persuasion.

A light form of coercive persuasion is television advertisements. Marketers often take advantage of the fact that when you are watching television, your mind is in a mild state of trance. They associate their products with some positive imagery that is completely unrelated. For instance, some of the persuasive images used by them are of puppies, babies, and sex. However, sometimes there is nothing relating the products to the images. Advertisers often make their products appear better than they actually are by bending the truth ever-so-slightly. On their own, these kinds of persuasive tricks are not really effective. Advertisements, however, most don't include love-bombing, shame, guilt, or fear tactics. Even if they are used, they are at low levels. Outright deception is prohibited by several laws, and a majority of companies convey the truth while informing their customers.

In contrast to this, a cultic group will make every possible effort to recruit and retain its members. These groups make use of different persuasive techniques in unison. Such methods strip the victim's real personality and form a new, group pseudo-personality. There is no method to avoid information control, deception, and lies. The new members who join the group don't know very much about the group or its purpose, or their expectations from the group. People start investing psychologically, spiritually, and emotionally, sacrifice a huge amount of money and time, and get deeply involved in the organization. It gets very difficult for them to leave the organization. Former members often struggle to regain their sense of sanity.

Persuasive techniques of mind control are everywhere around us, from activists, authors, scientists, religions, politicians, corporations, to family and friends. So, the actual question you should ask is whether you are being persuaded by open access to information, research, reason, and facts. Or are you persuaded by deceptive and manipulative methods? Consent that is gained through fraud is not real consent at all. The methods used by cults are also used in several dysfunctional families. An individual in an abusive marriage often faces similar experiences as someone in a cultic group.

Mind Control vs. Brainwashing

Cults generally have the same basic patterns and ingredients, but there are various assorted styles and flavors of cults. Brainwashing has gotten refined into mind control since the Korean War and has become very common in the modern world. In order to be under mind control, an individual does not have to be subjected to any of the obvious abuses that are associated with brainwashing like be kept without sleep or food or be treated badly.

People learn in two different stages, the subconscious and the conscious. Even though some cults don't agree that there is a subconscious level that is their main aim. For instance, activities like church services or seminars that last for one to two hours, create and make use of boredom. The subconscious mind is unguarded when the conscious mind starts to daydream because of boredom. Then, we are open to receive any messages that are being fed to us. Although this modern-day technique of hypnosis is mostly undefined, it is a recognized technique of mind control. The individual enters a state of hypnosis or trance, as is understood by those who study cults.

When an individual is aware of whom the person is, it is known as brainwashing. For instance, the Americans were stuck in the Korean prison. The American boy can more easily work his way out of the situation and have an understanding of what had happened to him as he can recall where he was before his mind was changed through coercion. He can also identify the enemy who was involved in that "transformation" or "process."

Mind control is, however, done by someone that the person trusts. It could be a teacher of a seminar or class, or a minister, etc. It is very difficult to bring mind control to the attention of the victim as the techniques are usually very subtle. They cannot detect that someone else is controlling their mind as they think that they are in control of their behaviors as it happening completely out of their awareness. When they start to realize that they have traveled from A to B but is unaware of where B is, it then dawns upon them. Mind control alters their view of reality and the whole world as well. They might even go through their whole life, failing to realize that they have been under mind control. They continue to view the world in the way that was shown to them by the cult and continues to refuse that they are not in full control of their mind. They fail to realize that they need help, and thus, is most hard to help. They will continue to be under mind control until something forces the people like them who are in the same cult to examine their belief system critically.

How to Take Control of Your Mind

Almost everyone has a negative voice inside their head. It is a part of life. Dealing with the negative thoughts that plague your mind day and night can help you grow and improve yourself to become a better version of yourself. Negative thoughts are a bit more manageable during the day as you are distracted by responsibilities, family, and work. However, the thoughts get louder when the night rolls in. It might get difficult to stop feeling helpless when you lose control. They might show up disguised as anxiety, doubt, or fear. Your imagination can get triggered by just a single small thought, and that can get you tumbling into a whirlwind that could knock you off. However, you can alter your thought process.

You can take back control through mind control. Mind control can improve the quality of your life. You can take back control of your thoughts even though you might not be able to stop the initial trigger. Here's how you can get a grip on your thoughts:

- **Present moment mindfulness:** You require a mental support system when you are trying to take control of your thoughts. Present Moment Mindfulness can work fast. If you get caught in the whirlwind of negative thoughts, identify them, remove and replace them. Try to keep your focus on whatever you are doing at the moment. For example, if you feel your mind wandering off into a dark path while you are washing dishes, stop and notice your activity and tell yourself that you are washing the dishes. Feel the warm water and the soap bubbling on your hands.

- **Do a reality check:** When the cyclone of negative thoughts gets a hold on your imagination, you start believing whatever you are thinking. However, in reality, it is just what you have created in your mind. It's up to you to remove your thoughts and bring yourself back to the real world.

- **Erase and replace:** At times, it is just enough to remind yourself to "erase and replace." This positive mantra helps to create room for positive thoughts by kicking out the negativity. Having a "replace" statement ready for use might also help you when you need it. You just need one word. It could be "go," "no," "stop," or whatever you would like. Repeat the word over and over again. You can be as creative as you wish—you can sing it, scream it, or chant it.

- **Name it:** When you feel stuck in a negative thought cycle, stop the cycle by naming it. Naming it creates a distinction in your subconscious mind whether you choose to say it out loud or whisper it. This will help to break the cycle.

- **Always be prepared:** Being aware helps you to be mentally strong enough to fight off negative thoughts. When you are aware, you can identify the triggers and immediately knock them off. You can take back control by being more aware and grabbing hold of your mind.

Advantages of Mind Control

Mind control is a very effective form of persuasion. It is exponentially more accurate and powerful than other methods of persuasion. One of the most important advantages of mind control is its effectiveness, power, and strength. Mind control is the best method of initiating a change of thoughts in another person. You could argue and debate with someone the whole day, but it might not alter their opinions. People tend to be a lot more irrational than they might care to agree and, in several cases, have a psychological immunity towards reasonable thinking and facts. Moreover, emotions play a more important role than rational and intelligent thinking. People tend to make decisions based on their emotions and then try to justify them by using rational thinking. Mind control allows you to appeal to their minds as well as their hearts.

Chapter 10: Techniques and Secrets of Dark Psychology to Influence People

Now, the reason why dark psychology techniques are efficacious lies in the way they interact with your psyche. The human psyche is structured in such a way that it is capable of filtering out stimuli that somehow don't conform to the patterns, beliefs, and values that permeate the psyche. For instance, if you believe in peace, your mind will reject any notion of violence. By the same token, if your mind is centered on greed and avarice, you may place minimal restrictions on schemes aimed at getting money. However, the subconscious mind, the layer that exists beneath the conscious mind, is unfiltered but equally able to process the stimuli that enter it. This is why the manipulator's true goal is to access your subconscious and implant ideas at that level. When that happens, the chances of ideas and beliefs sticking are very high.

This is why advertising is so repetitive. Think about it. If you only hear an advert once, the chance of you recalling it would be very slim. However, if you hear adverts over and over, there will come a point where your conscious mind will stop putting up a fight. When that occurs, the message can seep through into your subconscious. This is the secret of brand positioning. So, if you think advertising, at least good advertising anyway, is about selling stuff, guess again. Good advertising is all about getting you to think about a brand or a product constantly.

The Door in the Face

Directly from the experience of door-to-door salespeople, I present the technique of the door... in the face! When we want to obtain a certain result from our interlocutor, we should request that we consider too high and unreasonable: this request will undoubtedly be followed by a metaphorical door in the face, that is a refusal; at this point, we should immediately follow the real request that we had in mind: compared with the first, in fact, the new request will appear more modest and reasonable.

This technique bases its effectiveness on the natural tendency of our minds to make comparisons. If we provide the right term of comparison, no request will appear excessive.

This technique works because it arouses in the person a sense of guilt and an idea of concession. In other words, your renunciation will be perceived as a concession and then, it is a sneaky application of the "reciprocity rule."

Foot in the Door

This tactic is implemented in increments. This begins with the manipulator asking for small favors. Every time the victim complies, the manipulator will ask for increasingly bigger favors until they get what they ultimately want, or they exhaust their victim. At that point, the manipulator needs to move on to a fresh victim.

Consider this example:

A manipulator wants a large sum of money. Yet, they know they won't get it if they just ask for it. So, they ask for a tiny sum. Then, they pay it back. Next, they ask for a bigger sum and then pay it back. They do this as they build up trust capital until one day. They get what they want, never to be heard from again.

This example clarifies why this technique is called put your "foot in the door" and make room with your whole body...

A more rudimentary approach consists of asking multiple people for money with no intention of paying it back. Eventually, they exhaust the people around them. So, they need to move on and find new victims.

"Yes-Set" Technique

The technique of the "yes-set" consists of asking several questions to the interlocutor, for which they can only agree and answer "yes." This will create light conditioning that will also make them answer yes to your real request. It is a short-term freezing effect that causes the person to enter into a certain response perspective.

4–5 harmless questions in the preamble are enough.

For example, you want to watch a specific program on TV, knowing that the choice of your partner will probably be very different:

YOU: It was nice today, huh? It feels good to get some sun!

HIM/HER: Yes, it was.

YOU: Are you watching TV tonight?

HIM/HER: Well yes, I think so.

YOU: Remember the movie we saw the day before yesterday?

HIM/HER: Yes.

YOU: I liked it. He was practically the main actor, right?

HIM/HER: Yes, he was.

YOU: Do you agree to watch the 1:00 movie tonight? I think it'll be okay.

HIM/HER: Yes, if you want, what is it?

A funny little demonstration of this principle that I'm sure you already know. Ask someone to repeat the word "white" 10 times, and then ask the question "What is the cow drinking?" The wrong answer will have been conditioned by the earlier repetition.

The mechanism behind this technique is based on the use of "rhetorical questions" or statements that are true, taken for granted, or otherwise verifiable in the direct experience of the person.

In these cases, the person "leading" the report prepares the ground with a series of questions to which the interlocutor will surely answer yes and that is why it is called "Yes-Set."

And in all three cases, some truisms or true and/or verifiable statements are followed by an "unverifiable statement" which is an induction (or command) or a demand taken for granted.

Linguistic Presupposition

Some very insidious communicative maneuvers consist of asking the interlocutor questions to which it is not possible to answer simply with a "yes" or a "no," but that trigger in the subject of the actions as an answer to a command. For example, if I ask a person if they "can turn off the light, there on their right?" apparently, I am asking if they can do it, but in practice, I will get the switch off, which is actually what I wanted.

In other words, through the linguistic form of "embedded commands," you can skillfully camouflage a command into a question, as in the following example: "Do you want to tell me to know what's bothering you or would you rather wait a while?"

With this sentence, I create in practice an alternative through the construction of more proposals, where I take for granted that in any case, the subject will reveal to me what worries him.

The Linguistic-Presupposition is one of the most powerful and easy-to-use tools to give someone "apparently" a choice and at the same time "trap" them inside your idea, almost without any way out.

Bind is a hypnotic technique used to force a choice with words. It is also called the "illusion of alternative."

Let's see some examples:

- "After you go to buy bread, could you come by the newsstand and buy me the paper?"

- "When are you going to take me to the movies?"

- "Have you decided which foreign country to take me to for our anniversary?"

Each of these questions already provides a choice, and the trick is to take for granted a fact that is slightly hidden.

Reverse Psychology

This technique consists of assuming a behavior opposite to the desired one, with the expectation that this "prohibition" will arouse curiosity and therefore induce the person to do what is really desired. For instance, when you tell a child not to do something that is the first thing they do. This type of response persists throughout a person's life.

It's a way of getting things done, giving the opposite of the command you want to give. If I say things like, "don't be offended," "don't worry," I get the opposite effect, I will make my interlocutor stiffen.

Some people are known to be like boomerangs because they refuse to go in the direction, they are sent but take the opposite route. This type of behavior can be used by a dark persuader because it is a weakness that the victim has. Take an example of a friend who loves to eat junk food at any opportunity they get. The dark persuader knows this and therefore will suggest that they should eat healthy because it will be good for them, knowing that the friend will choose fast food anyway.

When individuals are told that they should not believe one thing or the other, they will pay closer attention to it.

Consider this situation:

You are looking to force your employees to work overtime without questioning it. However, getting them to log the hours can be challenging as no one is keen on staying beyond their usual shift. So, you really can't do much to convince them to work overtime. Then, you get an idea: Why not ban overtime? That is, anyone who wants to work overtime cannot do so. The justification behind it is that since no one wants to stay longer hours, then there will be no overtime. In fact, you could take it a step further and hire temp workers to fill in the extra hours. Now, your regular staff is concerned that others are encroaching upon their jobs. In the end, you may get resistance from your usual staff who are now demanding to work overtime in order to get rid of the temp workers.

In the end, you have successfully manipulated your staff to work overtime. You were able to play with their sense of security by banning overtime and then bringing other workers to cover the hours they wouldn't.

A convention playbook would have sought to incentivize workers so they would be more willing to stay longer hours. But this would have meant paying more or offering greater benefits. In the end, your manipulation attempts were successful without conceding any additional benefits.

Negative Hidden Commands

A negative hidden command is a specific linguistic model of reverse psychology in which instruction is formulated negatively so that it is perceived by the unconscious mind, bypassing the "critical guardian" of our interlocutor.

An interesting aspect of the unconscious mind is that, compared to the conscious one, it does not understand negation. This happens because our mind works by images and because there is no mental representation of the word "not." Therefore, the unconscious does not perceive it. In other words, our brain cannot deny experiences related to the senses without first visualizing them.

Chapter 11: Influence Everyone Secret

There are many times when the human mind is pretty easy to influence, but it does take a certain set of skills to get people to stop and listen to you. Not everyone is good with influence and persuasion, though. They can talk all day and would not be able to convince others to do what they want. On the other hand, some could persuade anyone to do what they want, even if they had just met this person for the first time. Knowing how to work with these skills will make it easier for you to recognize a manipulator and be better prepared to avoid them if needed.

The first thing that we need to look at is what persuasion is. Persuasion is simply the process or action taken by a person or a group of people when they want to cause something to change. This could be concerning another human being and something that changes in their inner mental systems or their external behavior patterns.

The act of persuasion, when it is done properly, can sometimes create something new within the person, or it can just modify something already present in their minds. There are actually three different parts that come with the process of persuasion including:

- The communicator or other source of the persuasion
- The persuasive nature of the appeal
- The audience or the target person of the appeal

All three elements must be taken into consideration before you try to do any form of persuasion on your own. You can just look around at the people who are in your life, and you will probably be able to see some types of persuasion happening all over the place. Experts say that people who are good leaders and who have good persuasion powers will utilize the following techniques to help them be successful:

- Exchanging
- Stating
- Legitimizing
- Logical persuasion
- Appealing to value
- Modeling
- Alliance building
- Consulting
- Socializing
- Appealing to a relationship

The above options are all positive ways that you can use persuasion to your advantage. Most people will be amenable to these happening. But on the other side, there are four negative tactics of persuasion that you can do as well. These would include options like manipulating, avoiding, intimidating, and threatening. These negative tactics will be easier for the target to recognize, which is why most manipulators will avoid using them if possible.

Now, you can use some of the tactics above, but according to psychologist Robert Cialdini, six major principles of persuasion can help you to get the results that you want without the target being able to notice what is going on. Let us take a look at these six weapons and how they can be effective.

The 6 Weapons of Influence

Reciprocity

The first principle of persuasion that you can use is known as reciprocity. This is based on the idea that when you offer something to someone, they will feel a bit indebted to you and will want to reciprocate it back. Humans are wired to be this way to survive. For the manipulator to use this option, they will make sure that they are doing some kind of favor for their target. Whether that is paying them some compliments, giving them a ride to work, helping out with a big project, or getting them out of trouble. Once the favor is done, the target will feel like they owe a debt to the manipulator. The manipulator will then be able to ask for something, and it will be really hard for the target to say no.

Commitment and Consistency

It is like humans to settle for what is already tried and tested in the mind. Most of us have a mental image of who we are and how things should be. And most people are not going to be willing to experiment, so they will keep on acting the way that they did in the past. So, to get them to work with this principle and do what you want, you first need to get them to commit to something. The steps that you would need to follow to get your target to do what you want through commitment and consistency include:

- Start with something small. You can ask the target to do something small, something that is easier to manage the change before they start to integrate it more into their personality and get hooked on the habit.

- You can get the target to accept something publicly so that they will feel more obligated to see it through.
- Reward the target when they can stick to the course. Rewards will be able to help strengthen the interest of the target in the course of action that you want them to do.

Social Proof

This is another one that will rely on the human tendency, and it relies on the fact that people place a lot of value and trust in other people and in their opinions on things that we have not tried yet. This can be truer if the information comes from a close friend or a person who is perceived as the expert. It is impossible to try out everything in life, and having to rely on others can put us at a disadvantage. This means that we need to find a reliable source to help us get started. A manipulator may be able to get someone to do something by acting as a close friend or an expert. They are able to get the target to try out a course of action because they have positioned themselves as the one who knows the most about the situation or the action.

Likeability

We all know that it is easy to feel attracted to a certain set of people. This can extend to friends and family members as well. So, if you would like to get others to like you and be open to persuasion from you, you first need to figure out how to go from an acquaintance to a friend. This will work similarly to the reciprocity that we talked about earlier, but some of the basic steps that you will need to follow to make this work include:

- **The attraction phase:** You need to make sure that there is something about you that instantly draws the other person to you.
- **Make yourself relatable:** People are more likely to be drawn to you if you are relatable to them in some way. It is also easier to influence another person if they consider you, their friend.
- **Communicate like a friend:** Even if the two of you are not quite friends yet, you will be able to make use of the right communication skills so that the target will associate you as a friend.
- **Make it look like you are both in the same groups and that you are fighting for the same causes:** This can make it easier to establish a rapport with them.

Authority

If you want to make sure that you can influence another person, then you need to dress and act the part. This means that you should wear clothes, as well as accessories, that will help you look like you are the one in command. Some of the ways that you can do this include:

- Wear clothes that are befitting to what people will perceive an authoritative figure would wear.
- When you communicate with the target, you need to do so in a commanding fashion.
- Make sure that you can use the lexicon and the language of experts in that field.

When you can position yourself as the authority figure, people will look to you for the answers that they need. It does not matter how well they know you or not. You will have a great opportunity to influence them the way that you want them to behave.

Scarcity

The last weapon that you can use for persuasion is known as scarcity. Humans like the idea of being exclusive and are drawn to anything that they are not necessarily able to find anywhere else. When you make something exclusive, you have a chance of making it appear more valuable. People are also going to become fearful when something they desire starts to disappear. This whole idea is part of the supply and demand principle. If you have something abundant, then it will be perceived as having a lower value and cheap. But if it is rare, then it must have a higher value and be more expensive.

This can work for human beings and products in the same way. Some things that you should keep in mind when you want to use the scarcity principle with persuasion include:

- Always imply that the thing you are offering is not going to be available to the target anywhere else.
- If you can, it is a good idea to implement a countdown timer on what you are offering. This gives a physical indicator to the target that what you are offering is truly going to disappear.
- You should never go back on the stipulations that you said in the beginning. You need to make sure that the target knows that what you offered is scarce, or this method is not going to work very well.

All of these principles can be effective ways for you to be able to use persuasion to manipulate your target. It is important to learn how to use them all and to do so in a covert way so that your target is not able to realize what you are doing.

When you are successful with bringing all of this together, you are sure to get the results that you want each time.

Chapter 12: Effective Communication Skills

Importance of Communication Skills

They are the most important skills that can help you develop and keep friendships and build crucial social networks. Communication skills can also help you take care of your needs while at the same time being appreciative of the needs of other people. It is common knowledge that no one is born with good communication skills, but like all other skills, you can learn them through trial and error by practicing daily.

Areas of communication that you have to practice regularly include:

- Conversation skills
- Assertiveness
- Non-verbal communication

Point to Note

There are many aspects to effective communication, and you may want more help in specified areas such as providing feedback, dealing with conflicts, and learning how to present.

Non-Verbal Communication

A large part of what people communicate to each other non-verbally. What you say to people with your body language or eyes is as important as what you utter. However, your tone of voice and body language does communicate messages to other people regarding your:

- Honesty (do you have any secret intention?)
- Attitude towards the listener (for example, contempt and submissiveness)
- Knowledge of the subject
- Emotional state or condition (for example, fear and impatience)

Therefore, if you are used to standing far away from other people, deliberately avoiding eye contact, and speaking quietly, you are simply saying, "Please stay away from me!" or "Please do not speak to me!" Sometimes, the chances may be that this is not the message that you wish to pass across.

Conversation Skills

One of the most challenging things to do if you have social anxiety is initiating a conversation and keeping it going. It is normal to struggle a bit when trying to start a talk because it is not easy to think of the things to say. This is usually the case, especially when you are anxious. Besides, some anxious people speak too much, which may negatively impact other people.

Assertiveness

Assertive communication is the expression of your feelings, wants, and needs honestly while making sure that you respect those of other people. When you express your thoughts assertively, you prove that you are non-judgmental and non-threatening, and you are responsible for your actions.

Social skills concern the skills required to manage and impact the emotions of other people effectively. Even though this sounds like manipulation, it essentially initiates a positive emotion and gets others to manifest their emotions positively. In this way, emotional skills can be regarded as the ultimate piece of the emotional jigsaw. A revisit of emotional intelligence indicates that it begins with understanding your emotions, which is self-awareness competence. Once you have understood your emotions, the next step is to handle them in what is known as self-regulation. With managed emotions, you can use them to accomplish your goals in what is known as self-motivation. If you understand and handle yourself, you will begin to comprehend others' feelings in what is regarded as empathy, and eventually, you will influence them in what is regarded as social skills.

In this manner, social skills will include the ability to persuade and impact skills in others. Social skills will also include communication skills and conflict management skills. If you possess social skills concerning emotional intelligence, then you will also possess leadership skills. Change management skills are part of social skills, and building rapport is another social skill applied in emotional intelligence. One must also possess collaboration and cooperation competencies to become socially skilled within the context of emotional intelligence. Against this backdrop, the following is a detailed dialog of requisite competencies to build your social skills within the context of emotional intelligence.

Persuasion and Influencing Skills

The art of enticing others and convincing them to absorb your ideas is known as persuasion. People who are persuasive or have an impact will read the emotional currents in a situation and perfect what they are saying to appeal to the spur involved. Persuasion is a function of communication and personality, and this demands that you become an effective communicator who is empathetic to others. Winning over people involves trying to convince them to join your course. You must learn to sell your views as a salesperson would do.

Communication Skills

Good emotional intelligence requires good communication skills. Learn to listen to others and channel your thoughts and your feelings. Make the people around you understand what it is you are communicating and look for the full and open sharing of information. Part of communication skills will require that you become prepared to learn about challenges and not just want to receive good news. If you are a good communicator, you will handle challenging issues directly as opposed to letting problems compile. Ensure that the message you are packaging is appropriate and then register and act on emotional cues when communicating.

Conflict Management Skills

Conflicts are unavoidable and sometimes not predictable. Both at home and work, the art of handling and resolving conflict is important. Conflict management skills begin with becoming aware of critical tact and diplomacy and how these competencies can be applied to defuse emotive situations. If you are a good conflict manager, you will manage to expose disagreements and help resolve them. Most importantly, conflict resolution does not involve you dictating the solution; it is rather helping the affected parties identify the different opinions, fears, and shared understanding to craft a solution. The competence of conflict resolution entails deploying sharing of emotions to motivate debate and open conversation and lessening the underlying problems. When resolving conflict, more emphasis should be placed on the logical position, as this is often the shared understanding among the conflicting parties.

Leadership Skills

Emotional intelligence and leadership skills are connected in multiple ways. The ability to influence requires that you tune your emotions and those of others to win them over. Influence is a critical attribute of good leadership. It is sometimes called charisma, but leadership skills involving influence go beyond charisma to match good emotional intelligence. The competencies of good leadership require you to articulate a vision and those other people with it. You do not have to be in a formal leadership position to give leadership. While holding your colleagues accountable, support and direct their performance. Learn to lead by example.

Change Management Skills

Change catalysts can be effective managers, individuals that make positive change while involving everyone. For all people involved, change tends to create pressure, partly because of the fear of the unknown. Good change management requires turning change into an exciting opportunity rather than a threat. Change catalysts recognize the importance of change and remove barriers. Change catalysts disrupt the status quo and advocate for transformation. Leading by example is a common attribute of change catalysts to trigger desired adjustments.

Building Rapport

It is important to create and maintain constructive relationships with other people. Mastering this skill will lead to improved relationships and an increased ability to work and succeed in life. People who are good at building bonds are great networkers, create and sustain a robust network of connections and contacts. Creating a rapport involves establishing relationships to keep it healthy. If you exhibit good rapport as a competence, then you are likely to have many friends. The essence of bonding is valuing others and taking an interest in their lives and being eager to learn more about them.

Team-Working

People with good collaboration skills will build good and useful productive working and other relationships, and some people function well with others. All these attributes are vital when building social skills in emotional intelligence. People with collaborative skills will see relationships as critical as the pending task and will value people as much as they consider the activity at hand. If you have collaboration skills, you will actively cooperate, share ideas and plans, and work with others to create an improved product. The best environment will attract other people to contribute. If you possess the competency of collaboration and cooperation, you will actively seek opportunities for cooperative work. A team will perform better when good team-workers are present in the group and this tends to attract other members to join the team. Good team-workers help the team build an identity and foster commitment.

Chapter 13: Brainwashing

Defining Brainwashing

Brainwashing refers to thought reform. It involves several different techniques that, over time, sway a person to change their very thoughts, feelings, behaviors, and core beliefs. They change so much that they have essentially lost their ability to make free choices; they become obedient. The techniques that cause the change can vary greatly, but as a general rule, when brainwashing has occurred, it is typically combined with some sort of danger and threat, with force frequently used.

This complex brainwashing enigma is essentially the gradual process of replacing the ideas of a victim with a manipulator about their being, and of replacing them with new ideas that should adapt to one's own needs, and that can either narrowly take place. For example, a manipulator can control a person or adopt the same principle but a broad group. The circumstance of brainwashing is like the one where people believe they can be a call for a higher purpose to join a terrorist organization. In the majority of other scenarios, indoctrination appears to be effective. Most believe that brainwashing is the Hollywood fiction of someone who continually imposes certain concepts on their victims, and within a short period, the person becomes the manipulator for every bidding. More realistically, it is a process that generally changes an individual's perception of reality far from what they have had a very gradual but voluntary process. The fundamental trick is to make the victim feel as though they are always in control. Several situations make brainwashing possible, and often they are motivated differently by it. Let us discover these specific scenarios, starting with the situation of a cult. A cultic can be said to be an organization of people who often believe that one individual is considered as their leader in something larger than themselves. The leader is often characterized by their exceptionally great influence and very charismatic behavior on their followers. The question that we now try to ask ourselves is, why is brainwashing a culture in those contexts?

The Process of Brainwashing

The starting point of brainwashing is going to be the social circumstances and the mental state of the victim. This is going to be the foundation for the rest of the process, and if the manipulator is not able to figure this part out, then the brainwashing session just won't be successful. Brainwashing is not a process that is going to work out for everyone. It is going to require a good identification of a person who is looking for something or someone who has a void they are trying to fill.

Once the brainwasher has found their victim, either through the Internet or in person, the process of brainwashing is able to begin. Contrary to the popular image you may have in your mind about a brainwasher, this person is often going to come across as someone rational, friendly, and calm. Someone who seems to have their lives together in a way the victim wishes they could have their own. Imagine how it would feel if you were homeless and a celebrity you admired befriended you. This is often how the process of meeting the brainwasher is going to feel for the victim.

The brainwasher is going to get to work right away. The first step for them is to create a level of rapport and trust between them and the victim. This is going to be done with superficial and deep similarities. The superficial similarities could involve some surface-level preferences, something like enjoying the same food or sport as the other person. They will then move on to a deeper level of rapport, some that could involve a deeper shared experience that they had in the past. The brainwasher will most likely convincingly fake these in order to create these bonds. So, if the victim shares with the brainwasher that they lost a close relative in the past, then the brainwasher is all of a sudden going to have a story that is similar to share with the victim.

This false connection and warmth emotionally are not the only thing that is going to occur. The brainwasher wants to cement the new bond as quickly as possible. It is not uncommon for them to provide favors and gifts to their victim. They could then send them a gadget or some other item they may find useful. They may treat the victim to a meal. The point of doing this is to create a sense of gratitude and indebtedness from the victim to that brainwasher. This is going to soften up a lot of the resistance that the victim may experience.

After the resistance has been stripped away a little bit, the next step is a sort of utopian presentation. This involves the brainwasher slowly, and increasingly offers a solution to all the problems that the victim formerly opened up about. This is not a big hard push or sell. Rather, the brainwasher knows how to do this in an offhand and casual way to make sure they don't deal with any negative experiences by pressing the victim. This solution is always the personality, ideology, or cult that the brainwasher is working to make the victim convert to.

The victim is going to want more information and more understanding of the solution that the brainwasher hints at. The brainwasher may even withhold some of this information in the beginning, treating it as something that the victim needs to do some work to attain. The point of doing this is to push some motivation on the victim in order to seek out and accept the information they are eventually going to hear.

After the victim has had some time being spoon-fed snippets of this belief system, and they have shown they will respond well to them, the brainwasher is careful in order to reveal the right information at the right time. This is a concept that is called a gradual revelation or milk before meat. It includes the presentation of an easy-to-accept idea before the really controversial idea is revealed.

For example, if the brainwasher is trying to convert the victim over to religious terrorism, they would not just start with the terrorism part. They may initially start focusing on the fact that God loves the victim, something that the victim is likely to accept. The more objectionable ideas, such as God wants you to blow yourself up, are saved until much later in the process. Once the victim has accepted that last part, then this brainwashing session is at a point of no return.

At this point, you may be curious as to why the victim is still engaging with the brainwasher, especially when these more objectionable ideas start to become apparent. There are three main reasons:

1. The vulnerable victim has been worked on by the brainwasher. They feel a strong sense of liking the brainwasher, and they want to get the approval of the brainwasher.

2. The victim has invested some time, and in some cases, money, in the process up to this point. This is often known as the sunk cost fallacy. The victim is going to feel like it is a bad idea to throw away all the hard work and money they have put into the process as well.

3. During this process, the brainwasher has been amassing a lot of sensitive and secretive information on the victim. The brainwasher is often willing to hold this information over the victim to keep the victim on the right path.

How Brainwashing Occurs

Brainwashing has several different steps, despite being a somewhat simple concept. In order to brainwash someone, at least in the way that it was done to those soldiers who were studied carefully and extensively, there are twelve different steps. Each of these culminates to create a changed person.

Assault on the Individual's Identity

This challenges a person's identity. People are frequently beaten when answering their questions about their own identities and immediately contradicted afterward. For example, if asked their name, they may answer, get beaten, and then told a new name. They quickly develop doubt about who they are as people.

Guilt

The person being brainwashed is then exposed to massive amounts of guilt, being forced to believe that they deserve the treatment being given. It is incredibly important here to make the person feel as if everything is their fault, or if something does not work out just right, then it is on them, and they must feel guilty.

Self-Betrayal

This stage involves the brainwashed individual being systematically forced to denounce everything they held dear. Friends, family, religion, culture, and anything else. It essentially culminates in destroying the identity of the person being brainwashed.

Breaking the Individual

Eventually, the person being brainwashed recognizes that there is no escape. Without the hope of escape and returning to life, the individual is consumed by fear and the fear of being destroyed, rendering them unable to reason and oftentimes desiring death as quickly as possible.

Leniency

At this stage, when the prisoner or brainwashed individual is sure they will break, someone offers a tiny beacon of kindness. The tiniest of leniencies here create a new hope. This is paired with the manipulator insisting that if the person does as request, then everything can be put behind them, and the prisoner is willing to do so to escape destruction.

Compelling to Confess

At this point, the prisoner likely feels a need to confess all sorts of perceived crimes. The point is to cleanse the sense of self in order to allow for progression. The captor, of course, encourages this.

Channeling Guilt

The prisoners then begin to feel guilty for his or her very sense of self rather than for the crimes. Everything, involving their beliefs, their family, and their likes becomes a cause for guilt. As they are accepting the viewpoint of their captors, they become guiltier over themselves.

Reeducation

At this point, the past identity and everything that went with it is discarded by the prisoners. They are open to reeducation, learning to live with the captor's desires and expectations.

Progress

The more they begin to accept the captors' perspectives and beliefs, the more they are welcomed into society and treated as humans, encouraging them to continue on their path.

Final Confession

At this point, prisoners are given one last confession. They are speaking as the new selves that were created by the process and given the chance to clean themselves of their past identity.

Rebirth

Now, the prisoners are recognized as humans once more. They are rewarded for good behavior and punished if they do anything reminiscent of their past lives.

Release

With the process complete, the prisoners are released into the real world, where they are given their rights as humans, but always faced with scrutiny for their new identity, or their old identity, and they are questioned.

Chapter 14: Instant Rapport

Rapport is an important feature of our subconscious mode of communication. Securing a rapport means being on the same "wavelength" with someone, and ensuring you have an instant rapport with a person means you are hitting it off with them at the very first go. Establishing a rapport with someone is an essential part of communication, whether you are engaging with them in a personal or professional capacity. If you are able to build a rapport with someone instantly, from your very first interaction, the chances are that communication between the both of you will not be a lot smoother and more convenient, and it will even go on to help both of you get along well with each other in the longer run. After all, first impressions do make a huge difference in how we judge someone, right?

What tends to happen a lot of times is that even if we are conscious about our actions, we might not end up making a great first impression or building a good instant rapport with someone. This is the case because how instant rapport is formed is not just determined by what we say and how we carry ourselves, but it is also heavily influenced by our body language and a lot of non-verbal cues, which are not things we are always consciously controlling, or thinking about. But thinking about how to efficiently come up with some strategies involving these non-verbal cues and modes of communication would be very helpful and would certainly go a long way in improving your chances of building and maintaining instant rapport with the people you end up interacting with.

Why Should You Build Instant Rapport?

Here are some reasons why building an instant rapport is actually very important, even if you do not actively realize it at all times:

- **People like people who (tend to be) like them:** It has been proven in numerous social psychological studies that people actually like people initially who share a similar mindset and have similar likes and dislikes as they do. This is one of the reasons building an instant rapport is important. If you can provide someone with the assurance that the both of you share some common ground, to begin with, it will increase your chances of them liking you and being open to having a lengthier engagement with you. You do not have to be carbon copies of each other, no, but just sharing facts about how the both of you like the same band or have the same taste in books can be beneficial. Small details are very important in having a rapport with someone.

- **First impressions can be very crucial for interviews**: Imagine yourself appearing for an important interview. Even if you have ensured that you have studies all you could, and know all the information, and are equipped with all the skills that are required for the position you are applying for, you must keep in mind that in all probability, you are one among many, many people with the same knowledge and skill set, appearing for the same position. It might sound upsetting to see things from this perspective, but this realization will also help you understand what you can do to set yourself apart from others and make sure that you have a better shot at securing the job. First impressions are crucial when it comes to things like interviews because these are situations where you need to make a quick good impression. In this case, building an instant rapport will actually help you greatly in the longer run. If you succeed in doing that, it is obvious that the people who are interviewing you would take notice of you more and would likely remember the interaction they had with you more vividly, so, naturally, you will be one of the first choices that will pop into their mind when deciding from within multiple candidates with a similar profile.

- **Instant rapport building is also important for leadership positions:** This almost goes without saying, but when you are assuming a leadership position (especially if you are working with a slightly larger group of people), it is important that the people who are working in the team along with you actually like you. It is impractical and nearly utopian to expect everyone you work with to like you at all times, but forming a general likeability is important, as it will really keep you going through the many other, minor disagreements any team is bound to stumble upon eventually. While assuming any leadership position or even during you are pitching for yourself to take up a position of authority (say, if you are campaigning for a round of student elections in your college), it must never leave your notice that despite being a great fit for your role, you are also absolutely required to be likable for the others actually to believe that you are right for the role. This type of likeability is easy to achieve if you have mastered the art of how to build an instant rapport with someone. Plus, rapport building can also help you with getting your words through to people in a more amicable way so that the future chances of conflicts are also low. In this way, you can actually kill two birds with one stone.

Tips for Building Instant Rapport

Here are some tips on how to build an instant rapport, which is simple and can help you build a foolproof step by step process of how to actually build an instant rapport with someone, even (and especially) if it is the very first time you are interacting with them:

Check if You Have an "Open" Body Language

Yes, there is such a thing as open and closed body language! Having open body language is one of the first tips anyone would ever give you about how to communicate non-verbally effectively. An open body language shows that you are welcoming and are open to interact and listen to new people and ideas. It also shows that you are interested in engaging with others. Some tips for maintaining an open body language are to have uncrossed arms and legs, greater hand movements while speaking, and attentive facial gestures while listening to the other person speak. You can remember and use the "SOFTEN" technique to easily ensure that you have open and positive body language. This technique tells us to S- smile, O- open posture, F- forward lean, T- (stay out of their) territory, E- eye contact, and N- a nod to show understanding. Some of these points are described in more detail below.

Eye Contact Is Important

Eye contact is always important because it communicates that you are paying someone enough attention. Keeping any sort of initial awkwardness aside, it is a great practice to actively try and maintain eye contact with anybody you are speaking to. If you are meeting them for the first time and you are trying to establish an instant rapport with them, eye contact would go a long way as it would not just tell them you are interested in them, but they would also feel reassured because having such non-verbal modes of interaction actually takes the burden away from the person to speak each and everything out loud at all times. This way, it would also help them ease into the conversation they are having with you. But while maintaining eye contact, always keep in mind that there is a boundary between being interested and making someone uncomfortable with excessive and forced attention. Maintain eye contact, but remember NOT to be creepy!

Let Them Know You Are Listening

A lot of times, it is not enough to only listen to someone else, but you should also actively let them know that you are listening. Otherwise, if they are not aware that you are listening to them, they might feel that you are not interested in what they have to say and would cut down the conversation short. If you are meeting someone for the first time, this step is even more important because, between friends and close acquaintances, it is easier to communicate because you both would already know how you attentive without actually showing it, but it is unfair for anyone to expect an almost stranger to ace this level of understanding in initial exchanges.

A few ways in which you show that you are a good listener is to maintain eye contact, nod while listening (and yes, there are different nodding gestures to convey different things, so keep that in mind as well!), and of course, stay away from your electronic gadgets while you are listening to someone else. Actively keeping that distraction away goes a very long way in assuring the other person that you are really interested in hearing them out. You might be interested in what they are saying and actually want to google more details about the topic at that exact moment, but they would not know that and might feel like you are just checking your social media instead of paying attention to them. In such a case, just make a quick mental note to yourself to look it up later, and focus more on face-to-face communication.

Keep in Mind the Setting of Your Interaction

Not every strategy works in all situations. Keep in mind where you are meeting. Is it outdoors or indoors? Is it a restaurant or a meeting room? Is it during the day or the evening? How many people are around? How loud is the place? All these factors (and more) about the physical setting of your interaction should constantly inform your decisions of the strategy you are going to use to build an instant rapport with anyone else. Eye contact might be more important in a louder, more public setting, and open body language might be more important in an outdoor setting during the daytime, and so on. The one size fits all approach does not work very well in human interactions, so let that always guide you in figuring out how you can establish a connection with someone you are interested in.

Utilize Gestures Such as Smiles and Handshakes

Physical gestures are also very helpful. Make good use of gestures such as smiles, nods, handshakes, a pat on the back, or a side hug (only if the situation and the nature of your interaction permit that). This is another reminder of how actions speak louder than words in a lot of settings. Verbally asserting something might not help put it across as effectively as shaking hands in approval with someone's argument. Sometimes, physical gestures can, therefore, be a lot more assuring and can be very helpful in securing a rapport. But having said that, do only how much is appropriate for the situation.

Chapter 15: How to Extend Your Influence

Influencing without authority for project managers may be a critical task. Maintaining the cats requires a mixture of strong management of projects and communication skills. You'll master the foremost complex projects by combining that with influencing levers. There are five forms without authority to impact.

Expertise

Expertise is a crucial element. Technical knowledge is vital as various roles function together during a project. Once you operate during a cross-industry unit, the business experience is often crucial. Use your expertise to support your suggestions and requests. One definition of a project manager would be the constraints of a timetable to support a deadline.

Information

When exchanged, knowledge is that the best. Influence others by daily, clear, and concise sharing of data that you simply learn. As a project manager, you've got priorities and plans. Roles and responsibilities are often complicated in diverse working groups. The news may be a street. Do not forget to gather it and express what you learn now. Knowledge of stakeholders is vital information that project teams got to bear in mind about the most project sponsor.

Resources

The correct tools are an important factor for the success of the project. The excellence between success and failure is often the imaginative use of capital. Impact the program by providing examples. Influence capabilities by identifying the most results expected and recording the talents required to realize results. Influence citizens by managing the pressure of employment and goal problems.

Relationships

Know regarding people and build deeper relationships. This helps you to find out what you'll do. Prepare responses and behaviors for criticisms instead of shocks. You should apply for periodic rewards across deep, long-standing partnerships. Finally, there's also a way of camaraderie that helps people to unravel challenges together.

Attitude

The actions or how you perceive people is one of the foremost significant influencing factors. Be honest and direct–you have long been accepting a crack in your honesty. Don't waste people's time-be prepared and arranged. Knowledge and pressure interact, but not pain. Your voice tone, your word selection, and your recognition of inauspicious situations are often your strongest influence.

Authority

A statement on jurisdiction. Jurisdiction. Authority is certainly the foremost obvious way of influencing people. You'll set their course and goals if you control capital directly. There are a time and an area to use the influence of somebody else. As an example, if you can't overcome major resource dependencies, call the bosses. Yet, you probably did not attempt to fix it personally afterward.

Appreciate People

Gratitude is another huge influencer/leader/role model quality. Efficient leaders know the facility of straightforward appreciation for channelizing people in the right direction. An easy gesture like thanking people, appreciating the trouble they put into a project, or publicly praising their skills goes an extended way in inspiring their loyalty towards you. Always prefer to recognize the work or efforts of others and specialize in lifting them as glowing role models for others. Few things boost a person's morale than being presented as a sparkling example. This doesn't just make the person feel wonderful but also helps you reinforce what's the proper thing to try. Everyone wants to be appreciated and valued, and will, therefore, be motivated to try things as they ought to be done.

Another tip that will cause you to an endearing leader is that the ability to assist people to save face during a potentially embarrassing or awkward situation. The person will feel indebted to you all the time. They're going to feel a deep sense of gratitude that you simply helped them out of a difficult situation that successively inspires unwavering loyalty.

You can help deflect focus from the person's blunder. As an example, if someone says something they shouldn't have said erroneously or accidentally, quickly change the subject before anyone notices or pretend nothing huge happened.

Show Abundant Passion and Enthusiasm

Have the proverbial fire in your belly for whatever you are doing. This causes you to an irresistible influencer. People can tell the difference when leaders/role models do something only for the heck of it and once they are truly operating with endless reserves of passion. Seeing you demonstrate the proper amount of passion and commitment towards a project/cause lights others up too. This, in turn, grows your influence. It attracts others to figure with you in your undying quest.

Stay Consistent

Consistency and commitment may be huge influence catalysts. It accelerates your influence in a positive direction by revealing how dependable your actions. People that are reliable, steadfast and dependable earn greater respect and obedience than those people that constantly change their actions supported what suits them.

Keep your actions and words consistent. Stay according to the principles you create. Be consistent in your attitude, policies, and leadership pattern. Above everything, stay according to your efforts for fulfilling the team's goals. People that don't hand over are ready to attract many followers. Consistent folks are seen as reliable and are the well-liked ones to be trusted with brand-new projects, initiatives, and responsibilities.

Find Solutions

Solution providers are always more wanted than problem diggers. Your influencer invariably increases if you possess a solution-oriented mindset. People flock to leaders/role models who have a more solution-focused mindset and are capable of arising with ingenious solutions to the foremost convoluted problems.

Folks who use heuristic, constructively problem-solving skills, and path-breaking solutions are often people magnets. They become instantly dependable and likable for his or her innovative thinking and positive approach.

Chapter 16: Powerful Body Language Techniques

Here are how to change your emotional state inside to help aid in pulling off body language and facial feats to give better appearances. This will be essential on those days when you emotionally feel far from perfect. Although faces will be judged more than body language as there are still people who have awkward body language that is successful.

Seven ways to use body behavior to improve your body language, behavior, and mood fast:

1. **Sit up straight.** Studies have found that people who are sitting with better posture had better moods than those who were slumped. Slouchers were also found to use more words and phrases associated with being weak and felt less self-assured.

2. **Power pose.** The power pose was found by scientific studies to slightly increased levels of testosterone and increase confidence and self-belief in own abilities.

3. **Go for a walk or do some body movement.** Going for a walk takes us outside of our head and neuroses so will surely increase confidence and give us energy.

4. **Lower shoulders.** To be more relaxed and look less tense. In the experience of this author personally, you will feel instantly more relaxed.

5. **Smile and practice a genuine smile.** This becomes easier with experience to those who are of more of a moody disposition and take a while to smile.

6. **Vocal tonality.** Talk in a deeper voice from the bottom of your chest to sound more assertive.

7. **Don't look down or at the floor (including when walking).**

Mental Tips to Change Emotional State

- Breathe through the nostrils and purely focus on the sensation of breathing through the nostrils slowly (but not too slowly).

- Meditate on the transientness of a particular thought which may be negative. Use conscious thinking energy to focus on something else. Imagine and focus on the emotions of bearing in mind that everything will be fine ultimately.

- Do not hold onto daydreams or future wishes or how you want the future to go-meditate on the fluidity and transientness of life and the universe.
- Method acting. Pretend you are a movie character in a certain emotional state, do everything from behavior to gestures and mannerisms

Practicing Effective Body Language in Different Contexts

Dating

This is a very nuanced social context with regards to human body language and behavior which is quite different from most human social contexts; other literature and books are the places for in-depth guides for how to make a date go well. Body language and behavior need to be adapted and/or mirrored to the other individual in question depending on their body language, behavior, and speech. Energies can present themselves in various forms including masculine, feminine, and neutral forms. Though in regards to masculine energy it is recommended to men to appear confident but not pull to overly dominant stances or body language. There is an emphasis to show that you are interested and listening to the other person but also to be in the present moment in emotional flow and show humor and personal value. Eye contact is important but needs not to be too strong and focused so that you are not staring the other person down. Of course, at the start of the date, you won't be up too close and personal but with time you find both of yourselves moving closer inwards together which is a sure-fire way to show that you like someone.

General Socializing

Social settings outside of home and work are more complex and dynamic and are more about being in a natural state of flow with other individuals or a group of people. There are fewer constraints on body language and behavior to show politeness and composure though there are facets of body language that may hurt the interaction. We generally like people who show interest and likeability towards us, though not too much, and characters with positive emotional states with who we can engage in social ebbs and flows. Power and dominance stances and body language are to be avoided. Social nervousness or anxiety can be hidden by putting hands in pockets or behind the head if sat leaning back.

Business and Workplace

Fidgety and more raucous body language is to be avoided like wildfire. Facial expressions and hand gestures indicate that you are thinking about what the other is saying. This is the one context where you need to demonstrate a maximum interest in the other person, especially if you are involved with customer handling. Power stances and poses can be adopted but must not be done too strongly to avoid intimidating others. In trying to emphasize key points in meetings use hands and fingers to help describe and dramatize what you are saying.

Confrontational and Uncomfortable Situations

In these instances of more complex and often uncomfortable social interaction, the best approach is to be more on the passive end of the spectrum, but you don't want to be too passive or you may end up being used or leading the aggressor to carry on. Firstly, do not mirror the other agitated person and perhaps extend the inner palms outwards to face them to show you are in semi-passive mode and want to rectify the issue at hand. Hand movements pushing downwards gesture to indicate that you pacify but that you are not ultimately submitting to them and that you want them to calm down. It is also best to keep your distance and only use a moderate amount of eye contact, but keep your body facing towards them so you are not signaling you are about to wander away carefree. For non-aggressive confrontational situations (i.e., when being called into the manager's office for a misdemeanor); use body language to show that you care and want to rectify the situation. If you have to make small white lies, try to use hand gestures and head movements to indicate conviction in what you are saying. Prey hands or fingers adjacent to mouth or lips indicate you are reflecting on what they are saying.

Conclusion

As we end this book, here are some subliminal messages that are a very effective part of mind control and are a very crucial technique to learn if you want to persuade anybody effectively. Subliminal messages are so powerful that they actually exist all over the modern world, and most of us don't even acknowledge it. They can be found in marketing, movies, news, and far more. Finding out to utilize subliminal messages will help you effectively utilize mind control on individuals in the most masterful way. You will have the ability to persuade anybody into thinking and acting in the way that you desire for them to act, and you will have the ability to have any outcome you desire when you master this strategy. This is next-level mind control that lots of people take years to master, but you are going to learn to master it easily and efficiently with these actions.

Downsizing

This method is an incredible way to utilize subliminal messaging to get individuals to do what you desire them to do. Using this method will enable you to get individuals where you desire them to be easy. The method is virtually uncomplicated and is typically used in sales and other comparable scenarios. You can modify it to work for anything. Essentially, all you require to do is begin with a large request and scale it back as you are talking. For instance, let's state you want to get somebody to talk to you on the phone. You could start by asking to hang out and maybe go on a date together. As the conversation progresses, nevertheless, work your way backward and simply ask for a call. Because it is not as grand and intense as the original request, they are most likely to say yes. After all, a call seems to bear much less pressure than a request to go on a date, right? Once you have them on the phone, you can press for the date!

First Name Basis

People absolutely enjoy hearing their first names. It has a specific result on people that are not attained through practically any other name in any language. Utilizing someone's name is a sort of flattery that also confirms someone's presence. Individuals like knowing that they are recognized for the core of who they are, and they are far more likely to adhere to what you are asking if you are utilizing their given name regularly. You likewise wish to refer them to what you want them to be for you. Let's state you desire "John" to become your friend. You could say, "John, did you take pleasure in the video game last night?" and when he says, "Yeah, it was respectable!" you might say, "I agree, friend!" This associates them with being your pal and is most likely to encourage them actually to feel as though they are your pal as well. This brings particular perks, such as trust, that are required to use brainwashing and mind control, too effectively.

Flattery

Lots of people argue that flattery will get you nowhere, however, this is incorrect. Flattery will get you everywhere if you use it. Individuals are attracted to those who are naturally captivating, and part of being captivating is using flattery. If you take the time to charm those you are speaking to, they are more likely to react in your favor because you make them feel good. Something essential to acknowledge with individuals, nevertheless, is the level of self-confidence they carry. Those who have high self-confidence will like to be flirted with heavily since you are validating their greater sense of self-confidence. Those who have low self-esteem, however, will end up being uncomfortable and daunted if you flatter them excessively. It triggers them to feel as though they are being "buttered up" and makes them experience a conflict considering that they cannot relate to what you are stating.

Paraphrasing

Individuals love to be confirmed, and paraphrasing is a great way to verify them. When you paraphrase somebody, they feel as though you are listening to them carefully and that you are confirming what they are saying. This makes them feel good and develops a fantastic sense of connection between the two of you. This is an excellent way to create that connection and use it as a chance to develop trust between you and the person you are talking with while also discovering your way into their subconscious mind so that you can speak past their conscious mind and into their subconscious. This is how you will get optimal success with getting them to do what you want!

Nod a Lot

Nodding is gotten in touch with a favorable agreement between you and the person you are speaking to. Nodding frequently throughout the conversation, instills a very positive feeling into the person you are talking with and helps them feel as though you are truly listening to them. When they see you nodding and agreeing with lots of parts of the conversation, they are going to feel more likely to nod and also agree when it comes to your turn to talk. This creates a total positive scenario where you can easily get them to agree with you because the sense of "agreement" is high in the conversation in general.

Option Restriction

You wish to restrict choice without it being obvious that you are doing so. For example, instead of asking an individual the type of white wine, they would like, ask "red or white?" The second question will restrict them to either white or red. You will eventually get to select the white wine based on the color that they picked. They will not realize that you basically persuaded them to permit you to pick which red wine the two of you are going to consume. Giving individuals choices that distract them from the one choice that you do not desire them to make.

Making Use of Reverse Psychology

This is a method that is used by individuals to get what they want by asking or demanding what they do not want. Researchers use another term: self-ant conformity because your need goes against what you want. Another way that psychologists deliberate reverse psychology is through the term reactance. It is describing the unpleasant feeling that individuals get when they feel that their freedom has been threatened. The typical way to react to that risk is to the opposite of what has been required of you. It's the going against authority element.

Thank you for your support in this book!

www.ingramcontent.com/pod-product-compliance
Lightning Source LLC
Chambersburg PA
CBHW080628030426
42336CB00018B/3122